ELEMENTS OF MY SOUL

VIKKAS BHARDWAJ

VIKKASZONE

This book is a work of life reflections and poems. The account is from the author's perspective and memories and is represented as accurately and faithfully as possible.

Elements of My Soul @ 2022 by Vikkas Bhardwaj

979-8-9874358-0-9 Ebook

979-8-9874358-1-6 Trade Paperback

Interior design by: Lissa Woodson www.naleighnakai.com

Developmental Edits by Naleighna Kai naleighnakai@gmail.com

and Stephanie M. Freeman - stephaniemfreemanauthor.com

Beta Read by D. J. Mitchell and Kelsie Maxwell

Cover designed by: J. L. Woodson jlwoodson@woodsonstudio.com

www.woodsoncreativestudio.com

https://mrstaroftheworld.wixsite.com/vikkas

Cover Photo: Vikkas Bhardwaj for www.vikkaszone.com

ACKNOWLEDGMENTS

My first debt is to God. Goddess Durga has been my motivation since the beginning and Shivji is key inspiration to write through my spirituality and acknowledge "I am a speck of dust" in this vast universe, and we are all just minutest species living on this planet. Let go of your "EGO" in this lifetime and try to achieve moksha through your dharma and karma.

I thank you, God, for opening my eyes every morning and letting me see this beauty called life.

I want to thank my Mom and Dad for always inspiring and pushing me to achieve whatever my heart desires. My mom always tells me, "Life awaits you in abundance, my son." I lovingly thank my baby sister, Megha, for motivating me throughout and pushing me to go beyond my comfort zone.

I thank Vasant Vijay Maharaj, a renowned spiritual Guru from South India, who has helped me immensely understand life and the rituals of how to do something as simple as puja in a temple. This Holy man stayed in Himalayan mountains without any clothes for more than 10 years, has done intense meditation for 25 years in Varanasi, a holy city of India. He is a Siddha Guru from Krishnagiri, Tamil Nadu, India. His knowledge and wisdom about Goddess Durga is unimaginably beyond us humans. I am so thankful to him for teaching me the mantras and the process of enlightenment.

I'd also like to thank none other than World's Biggest movie stars— Mr. Amitabh Bachchan and Mr. Salman Khan. Besides Superman, Salman motivated me to work out and feel better about myself. I wanted his hairstyle and his body. Seeing his energy and his stardom back in the 90's enthralled me. Pushed me to work out, and I started going to the gym. I had the privilege of meeting him a few times. Admired him throughout. Mr. Amitabh is just an iconic father figure for all of us. He's an actor beyond time. His perfection and timing are what got and kept my attention. He also reminds me of my own father —what women would consider tall, dark, and handsome.

Without the support of an exceptional lady, USA Today bestselling author, Naleighna "Lissa" Kai, this book would not exist. Naleighna has always pushed me to start my own photo stock website Vikkaszone.com and embrace genres that I previously was not aware of. She has been encouraging me to publish my poems for years. Without her late-night efforts and working on this book on her lunch breaks, this would have never happened. She is not only my friend, but a great well-wisher who only wishes for my happiness. I am in debt, honored to have such a friend and a believer, I humbly thank her from my heart.

I also humbly thank #1 bestselling author, Stephanie M. Freeman, who did a developmental edit on this work. Her words are like pure gold, and the way she understands the written word is amazing. Thank you to D. J. Mitchell and Kelsie Maxwell for laying eyes on the project and giving insight.

I want to Thank Pamela Stanton for always standing by my side and sponsoring me to attend author events for all of these years. I am thankful for her support. DCL publications truly rocks and I am very grateful for them.

And to you, dear reader, for choosing this book to take a journey with me of understanding peace and joy, light and love. Thank you.

FOREWORD BY STEPHANIE M. FREEMAN

Poetry is the music of the soul. With one word or a thousand, a poet can capture the essence of the human condition or build cathedrals in the mind. Poetry reminds us that we are luminous creatures capable of inflicting great beauty and great pain. Whether written or spoken, words linked in rhythm and rhyme tell of our humble beginnings and a life well lived. Poetry reminds us of our frailty and our strength in the face of adversity.

I met Vikkas through a mutual friend, national bestselling author, Naleighna Kai, and had the opportunity to read some of his words and was blown away. With every poem and every passage, I caught a glimpse of the boy he was and the path he took to becoming the kind, compassionate, and considerate man he is today. His poetry and his story resonate with each word that he put to the page. His words are a unique kind of rugged magic that motivate, inspire, and comfort the weary and downtrodden.

His poetry… his story is just the kind of sustenance needed for the journey across the choppy waters of life to the safe harbor of home.

This book is dedicated to Devika Bhardwaj
My earth angel who is now watching over me from the spiritual plane . . .

DEC 2 ND
JAGARAN

Maa
MY WORLD

MOM WITH HER PARENTS ON THE DAY OF HER MARRIAGE

INTRODUCTION

Elements Defined

According to Hinduism, every human body essentially is made from five elements which are:

Earth (Bhumi), Water (Jala), Fire (Agni), Air (Vayu) , Space / Sky (Aakash) .

Hindus believe that, upon death; all these five elements of human body are dissolved to their respective elements of nature, so that it can balance the cycle of nature.

This book of reflections is put into sections that highlight these elements.

EARTH (BHUMI)

"Your soul is the essence of who you truly are. It is timeless, ageless and eternal." —Muses from a Mystic

MUMMA'S MEHNDI NIGHT DECEMBER 1
2022

1

AN OCEAN OF ELEMENTS

My journey of first love, betrayal, heartbreak, and the whispers of Bombay dreams are my spiritual journey to the infinite mind, body, and soul crafted in these pages. As in all things where there is happiness, there is also sadness, like clouds blocking out the sun. Darkness surrounds us from time to time, but I found comfort in pouring my soul upon the page.

With every word I write, I am reminded that my soul is like the elements as sure as the earth beneath my feet, the air I breathe, the fire that warms me, and the water that quenches and surrounds me. An ocean of elements, with light and love, like a lighthouse, leading the way. All that I am, or ever will be, is made up of those simple yet essential things and so are you, dear reader.

It is no mistake that my book found its way into your hands at this very hour and at this very moment. Perhaps you, too, have been at the mercy of bullies, heartache, or disappointment. As painful as these experiences were for me, they taught me great lessons that helped to make me the man that I am.

Where there was rejection, I learned to value self-acceptance. Where there was cruelty, I learned compassion. Where there was sadness, I learned to relish happier times. I learned to savor each moment for the miracle it was because life is fleeting.

I was certainly not immune to life's struggles. When I was a boy, the kids used to call me Gandhi because I had big ears. My only escape was Superman. Growing up on those iconic films and falling in love with that larger-than-life hero, Christopher Reeve portrayed, taught me a valuable lesson. Like me, this fictional character was the ultimate outsider. If he could persevere despite all of the odds stacked against him then maybe ... just maybe, I could too. And you know what?

I did.

Throughout my poetry-laced memoir, I will share snippets of what was going on in my life as I sat down to write. Perhaps you'll find yourself in that place of transition like I did when I moved from New York to California and Heaven, as well as the earth embodied in the form of my first love. Maybe you'll find yourself in the darker times of my life when tears were not enough to erase the pain.

Perhaps you'll find yourself in the stories I tell of my first love, my family, especially my mother and sister. Without them, I am absolutely nothing. My mother's name is Devi, which in Hindi means Goddess. That name fits her perfectly. Maybe one of my poems will remind you of your first love or a crush you built all of your hopes and dreams on, only to see it fade like autumn leaves.

Perhaps none of these things have crossed your path. If nothing else, I want share a bit of my life with you so that you understand exactly what happens when a boy like me goes through heartbreaks, and more importantly, how leaving the United States for nine months changed my life in ways I couldn't possibly imagine.

2

A LETTER TO LOVE

DEAR LOVE
    I ask, how are you?
    Dear love,
    When I fell in love
    Was that always true
    Love, you made me smile
    Love, you made me go into another dimension
    Love, you're so cute to have in your heart
    But love where do you go when two people are apart
    Are you full of yourself?
    Because you know you're so powerful
    You have authority to control others
    But love, why do you hurt sometimes?
    Love makes me want to hide and not show how I feel
    You like my tears when they fall
    Love, you're just a four-letter word
    That flies in my reality higher than a bird
    So love, tell me who discovered you
    Tell me love, you have died so many times in my mind
    It's like every time I committed a crime

So please don't leave love because I will always be looking for you
Just and FYI
Cupid's last thoughts to me
Love spelled backwards is e v o l
Or is it ... evolve?
Tell me, my love,
Because if it is
It's not worth it
I won't love at all

3
_____

I FOUND MYSELF

You lost me in the woods
   You taught me how to keep the fire alive
   You said to me never dive in the ocean of lust
   In the storms of life, we are all dust
   You gave me a locket of heart
   I opened it and found snakes
   You lost me, but I found myself
   A mind like yours
   Next in line to me
   Your million Lives
   All worthless for you to see
   You might as well leave
   Before your heart turns into desires of unknown
   A minor or infant what a child to be
   When he grows on the hands of life
   Will he be lost just like I was?
   But I found myself
   That's love

4

IT'S TIME TO CRY

WON'T YOU COME DOWN AND DECIDE
> Don't give us a ride inside your troubled mind
> Making us smell roses that carry poisonous bites
> It's time to cry

DECEIVING lovers as well as friends
> Put a spell on them so it all ends
> Makes them go blind trying hard to find
> It's time to cry

LET it rain through their eyes
> The wicked ones get trapped in soul ties
> The lips form the most indecent lies
> It's time to cry

WHEN THEY MAKE a wish on a falling star
> Playing the crying game

VIKKAS BHARDWAJ

Leaving the heart with a scar
Then they'll know, it's time to cry

WHILE I'M SLEEPING and dreaming,
They are dancing those fools
The pain returns and it's so cruel
Erasing the love and saying goodbye
It's time to cry

TAKING advantage of the unknown
Thinking that my mind is blown
The kind of pain that cuts to the bone
It's time to cry

I SHOULD HAVE THROWN you away
Like clothes that are well worn
Receiving no compassion since the time you were born
It's time to cry

YOUR DRAMA, I really don't want to see
Protecting all that is left of me
I've seen all your acts, no other way to be
It's time to cry

GO FIND yourself another school
Perform better next time, find another fool
I will no longer be used as a tool
It's time to cry

THIS LIFE CAN BE SO VERY sad

Embracing the love we never had
Turning the sorrows into something glad
Is it time to cry?

THE TEARS *dry up and now I can bloom*
Because there's a new clock in my room
And it says . . .
No more time to cry

5

INDIAN BIRD'S DESIRE

I HOPE YOU KNOW *I* AM ALIVE
Living well but soon to die
Without you

I MUST TOUCH *you*
Feel you
Waiting impatiently
Don't know how I'm breathing

I THINK *you know love is like a prison*
I'm blinded by your love with no reason
When I return just love me the way you used to

GENTLE EYES KNOW *everything*
I'm lost in the rainbow
Trying to find my special color
Writing this and the pain is getting duller

· · ·

CRYING *like a baby*
  Please let me shed some tears in your hands
  Kiss them
  Drink them
  Free them
  And you'll see the ocean that I'm drowning in

  Don't confuse water with tears
  Water dissipates
  Tears create fire
  Like sweet Broken Wings
  Of my Indian bird's desire

I SPEAK *the truth not the facts*
  I want you
  I need to be loved by you

I WANT *to run away with the night*
  Only if the stars could give me a ride
  Only if the clouds could bring me to you

CAN'T *anyone tell you how my emotions*
  Are hiding under the birds that once flew
  Free and happy

DYING *to listen to those secret words*
  You know what they are
  I love you

· · ·

VIKKAS BHARDWAJ

I'M WAITING *like a farmer awaits the rain*
   I want to be the lightning so I can strike away the pain
   I hope you know how I feel

MAYBE YOU DON'T
   A lover's cry like burning fire
   Is the heated temperature of
   My Indian bird's desire

WATER (JALA)

1

WORLD OF GOODBYES AND GALAXY OF HELLOS

HEARTBREAK RARELY PREPARES US FOR A WORLD OF GOODBYES OR THE galaxy of hellos that follow. Traveling over that alien, ragged terrain of a broken heart is a journey we all must take if we are to grow. Circumstances dictated that I travel with my family back to India. I was seventeen or eighteen at the time when my first ever girlfriend left me because she thought I was not coming back to the United States.

Some of the poems in this section of my memoir were actually written in India. The bitter sting of a first love lost flowed across the pages of a journal I kept. When spoken words escaped me, I found an ally and comfort in my pen. With shattered dreams crowded around my feet, this acquaintance with heartbreak left me in despair and seeking answers beyond the shores of the United States.

Finding a positive outlet is key. Others may choose different art forms. I chose my pen. Sometimes, making something out of nothing or the scraps that remain, serve as a reminder that if things fall apart, you have an opportunity to put things back together from a place of experience. No one ever said it would be easy. It certainly wasn't for me, but oh, the lessons I learned along the way.

Learning about love, girls, and relationships could have left me bitter, but with the love and support of my mother and sister, I realized that I could smile again ... love again. Getting to that place meant enduring the loss and navigating the backroads of grief to get to the other side. And that, dear reader, was something for which I was unprepared.

2

CRY BESIDE MY BODY

TEARS MADE UP OF INK
   Life goes by in a blink

WIND IS *like a passing angel*
   My eyes looking at heaven

BUT SEEING *shadows of you*
   Because you
   Cry beside my body

WHITE UNICORNS COMING *to take me*
   Into black jungles too dark to see

MY LOVE RUNNING *after your fragrance*
   Speaking words that aren't flagrant
                  • • •

VIKKAS BHARDWAJ

DIVE *into a well*
    Take me to a place where we can dwell
    Eternity

UNDECIDED *on where to be*
    Look at her and there is much to see
    Tell her not to cry beside my body

WHAT YOU KNOW

You know that when you pluck a rose
    You fall in love with it
    But what your eyes don't see
    The bleeding behind those thorns
    Dripping down into the soil

PETALS FALLING *off going back to the source*
    Their lover's calling but they don't hear
    Too filled with this thing called fear

SHE KNOWS *the sun shines*
    And the moon fades away
    But what she doesn't know is
    They do so from very far away

LONELY SOULS COME *out in the dark*
    Running to fight the wars

VIKKAS BHARDWAJ

> And we see each one of them
> As falling stars

HE'S DOWN *and fallen and she thinks it's love*
> *She will never know or have anyone better*
> *She searches, but misses what I had to give*
> *She just wants another heartbeat in order to live*
> *Some unnamed thing from someone else*

HEAVENLY ANGELS ARE COMING *and need time to release*
> *So they cover up*
> *But we can still see them beyond the dark clouds*

IS IT GOING TO RAIN?
> *Or is someone's tears falling?*
> *Either way, you won't know*
> *Until they come calling*

MYSTERIES TO SOLVE *or ones to behold*
> *Either way, you still won't know*

4

BURY ME DEEPER

DON'T YOU SLIP WHEN I FALL
  Put me in six feet of lined wood
  Put white satin sheets on top of me a
  Ad there'll be nothing for me to see

  My eyes closed forever
  Bury me deeper
  Thirteen feet under the ground
  Nowhere for me to be found

  My lovers calling my name
  Opening my sore eyes thinking it can never be the same
  Can't come back
  Can't be loved

MY APPEARANCE somewhere in the next life to be Duplicated
  I'm coming
  Place my lover's photo on my heart
  Place her gifts in my hands

VIKKAS BHARDWAJ

Place her love letters on my eyes
So my journey to Heaven can be a loving one

I WISH *to see the next rising sun*
Give me that last kiss on my lips
Touch me for a last time as time slips
Love me for the last unstoppable time
Time is forever
But I'm leaving you

TAKE *the last rose and place it on me*
So I can remember the way you smell
Your lover
Me

Don't be surprised

Don't be surprised

5
_____

DON'T BE SURPRISED

IF I COME FLYING WITH THE BLUE ANGELS
I am dressed in all white floating in front of your house
If you could only see me
You would be surprised

DEATH COMES SOON *to those who wait*
I know for our love I'm twelve centuries late
I want you to know
Don't be surprised

DON'T BE SURPRISED *to see me in your room*
The possibility to touch
I am there to only comfort you
I am sure I left this lonely world
Don't be surprised

I'LL BE HOLDING *a cup under your eyes*

So when you cry, your tears satisfy the thirst
Don't be surprised

WHEN I LEAVE *and if I don't say goodbye*
Make sure you thoughts take off and kiss the sky
Don't be surprised

FIRE (AGNI)

1

THE LADY IN WHITE

REJECTION IS A PECULIAR ANIMAL. ON THE OUTSET, IT MAKES YOU question your self-worth. In hindsight, I now see the blessing within the experience. My first crush in high school rejected me because, in her mind, I wasn't handsome enough. All these years later I can still hear her rebuff and her off-handed comment to a friend. She just looked at me and said, "Oh, no, I don't like him like that, you know."

Little did I know, that sometimes from the greatest sorrows come the greatest blessings. On that day, I discovered my spiritual connection to something bigger than myself. Spiritually, I've always been connected to the Universe, it seemed only appropriate that when I thought my world was at an end, my angel came and reminded me that while seasons end, all was not lost and that love, like spring, would bloom again.

The day my first crush broke my heart, I met my guardian angel. I was on my bike, taking the busy streets from my high school to home. While trying to manage the pain in my heart, I saw a woman dressed in all white. Have you ever met a person you felt like you've known your entire life? Well, that was the feeling that washed through me like a cleansing rain at the sight of her.

It had to be around four or five o'clock in the evening. Every move I

29

made brought me closer to home. She was the most beautiful thing, but also the scariest I've ever seen. Fear became a fire beneath my skin as I pedaled faster, not sure if I was seeing things or if I was actually in the presence of an angel. We've all heard the stories about being kind to strangers because we could be entertaining angels. but as a kid you shrug away those stories.

I remember rushing through the streets, not caring if the cars rushing by were going to hit me. My conscience replayed all of the mischievous things all kids do. By the time I reached my house, I was in sheer panic mode. I tossed the bike aside, ran to my bedroom, hid under the sheets, and began to pray. *What have I done? What have I seen? What is this? What is this, God? Is this my time to go? Is this like, what's going on?*

I have had out of body experience while sleeping at night. I was awakened or in that state where I felt I was up but was not. Must have been three in the morning or so. My body was stretched out on the bed, but I felt my soul leave my body and actually pass my house, reach the top of the sky and pass earth to a different dimension. It was the most surreal feeling I have ever experienced, it is like your soul in a U shape and being sucked by a force unknown all the way to the top. Before I could even thinking about yelling or screaming, I realized that I could not. Only then was I awakened and physically got up from my bed and wondered what that feeling was. I have read about astral travel. This was the second time it has happened in my life.

Another time when I was sleeping, I had a saint wake me up and said tap on earth (meaning, tap my foot on the ground). When I complied, my soul again got sucked in that familiar U shape of air and went all the way to the top. And a saint, dressed in all white, told me this is the pathway to god. When I looked at him, I asked, "So when I tap my foot on earth and meditate, this leads to god?" He said, "Yes." Before I knew it, I was sucked back into this life and on my bed. I woke up with a beautiful feeling. I always feel angels around me; energies around me as I can sense a lot of things.

From an early age, seeing my parents pray and tell us about our temple and the gods and goddesses we worship. We were taught that from birth to our eventual death, Brahma, The Creator, Vishnu, The

Preserver, and Lord Shiva, The Destroyer, are essential to our very existence. I've always had a closer spiritual connection to Lord Shiva in particular, His teachings are a constant source of comfort that I relied on as a boy. As I lay there praying, the wisdom of Shiva rained down on me, and I realized that while I may have been rejected and my illusions of a relationship with my first crush were destroyed, Vishnu preserved me from further hurt, harm, or danger on my reckless journey home. Each of them, like the elements of my soul, worked in tandem to prepare me for the next leg of my journey.

They still do.

2

MAKING LOVE WITH HEAVEN

SITTING ON THE HARPS AND IMAGINING TO PLAY
    Dancing with the angels what words can't say
    Heaven is too far but I'm too close
    Like two Thorns stuck in a Rose
    Blood like sugar on the tip of my tongue
    Nice lady dressed in white
    This is what she sang:
    If you make love with Heaven
    You'll create Mysteries

WAKING *up to see a nightmare*
    Being sacrificed by God's tears in my ears
    Voices are like footsteps in my brain
    Look outside, is it the rain?
    Not possible
    Foolish soul like me thinking, it's music
    Is it my time to leave?
    Is he trying to take me away?

I know Heavens caretaker is crying
Please don't oh powerful one
I won't ever love again
Until eternity
A fading smile ....

3

ANGELS WATCHING OVER ME

THINKING BACK ON MY ENCOUNTER WITH MY ANGEL, I AM CONVINCED that Lord Shiva sent her to comfort and watch over me. While I longed to talk with my father about my experience, I understood that he was always busy providing for the family. Back then, I didn't have a close relationship with my dad. Our relationship became stronger before I moved to Bombay to work as a model and also work in films.

He is the most supportive father anyone could ever have. From him, I learned the importance of duty, honor, and how to take an active role in caring for my family financially, spiritually, and emotionally. Every aspect of life is a lesson custom-made to make me a better man.

Armed with that knowledge, I took all of my experiences, dreams, desires, and heartbreaks and put them into my poetry and video photography. Through the arts, I learned to appreciate and cultivate my four passions: education, my relationship with my family, my spirituality, and my heart.

Some of the most profound spiritual experiences that I've had since seeing my angel came to me in the form of dreams. Visions of Lord Shiva, with the trident in his hand, and the Goddess Durga, like benevolent shadows ordered my steps as they both enchanted and encouraged me.

But the lady in white still frightened me as a kid, but writing it down in my journal and sharing it with my Mom was my saving grace. She read my halting, awkward ramblings of a novice poet and with a wealth of compassion and her signature all-knowing smile, she gave me an answer that settled in my spirit.

"It must have been an angel looking over you, son."

Today, I would interpret her words as: *Fear not, my son. In your greatest agony, your soul called out for her. She brought you safely home and she stays with you still. There is no reason to fear.*

My mind is stuck in the past, my body is here in the present, and I can't imagine a future.

Our world was changed on December 8, 2022. My goddess, my mother transitioned. My father and my sister are broken to pieces as she was the foundation of this house. Hundreds and hundreds of people are coming to our house to grieve and meet us. After cremation on the 13th of December, her soul is detached from this physical body.

37

She will be my angel and will never leave me as she had promised me long ago. Most loving, kindest and giving soul anyone ever had the pleasure of meeting.

She was a gift from the goddess sent to us in this lifetime.

I am trying hard to move on but can't come to reality that she is actually gone. A few days after she passed, there was food left on the kitchen table and we were about to sleep. All of sudden we heard the sound of something falling on the ground. We ran downstairs and a long metal spoon was on the floor. That was mom! She told us to put the food in the refrigerator. That never happened before where a metal spoon just sitting on the table falls on the floor by itself.

I came away from that experience with the Lady in White and others throughout my life with the understanding that even in the depths of despair there are diamonds to be found.

I came away from the experience of my mother making her transition with a different set of lessons. I can sense her, feel her, and know that she will never, ever leave us. We pray for her moksha and to be at the feet of the goddess as she took her away so soon. She was a gift from the goddess sent to us in this lifetime.

We all start off as lumps of coal hidden deep in the earth. Lessons, adversity, and great pain are the pressure points that give us the kinds of facets that make us who we are and just what the world needs.

4

BLACK DRESSED ANGELS

A STEADY ROCK MOVED BY YOUR VISION
   A bad-tempered lion died by my illusion
   Make space for me
   Breathe when you die
   Trying to fly with your feet mired in clay
   Please don't cry, there is more to say
   The biting of fearsome snakes nobody hears
   Sunlight from Heaven
   Destroyer convincing the destroyed
   Stop this insanity
   Black dressed angels

5

THE PEEPAL TREE

Life comes in phases and with each stage I've entered, there were new challenges to overcome and other gemstones, like wisdom, I discovered would color and shape not only my life but the lives of everyone around me. While some challenges were daunting, others were downright frightening.

While living in the United States, my family moved from Artesia to Pomona. In Hindu culture, we have a halting respect for trees. In our legends, ghosts and spiritual beings live in them for centuries. We believe in the power of the trees and what lives within them. The roots of certain, special trees go down and beyond the Earth's surface. They burrow very deep, in places that science can't measure. One of them is called a Peepal Tree.

The tree itself is of the fig species and can often be identified by its uniquely heart-shaped leaves. What makes the tree unique is that the leaves seem to move without the aid of a warm breeze moving through the canopy.

Buddhists and Hindus alike worship this Tree of Knowledge because of its intimate connection to Brahma, Vishnu, and Shiva. Each of them represents parts of this sacred tree. For anyone to cut down such an embodiment of this holy aspect of our lives is not a thing to be taken lightly.

When we returned to the states and took up residence in Pomona, California, my sister's bedroom window was open one night. She actually felt footsteps or a hand on her bed, like something was walking on the bed. She told me later that she thought it was me or our mother coming in to say good night to her. I'm very close to my sister, I hug her and kiss her cheeks all the time and the idea of her being in danger of any kind hurts me to my very core.

She couldn't see anyone, but still felt a warm breath on her neck. She started chanting Lord Hanuman Chalisa, a mantra that keeps the ghosts away. They call him the monkey god, but we call him Shree Lord Hanuman. She chanted and after a couple of seconds, the breathing stopped. Whatever being that was in her room went away. She ran to my room, opened my door at two in the morning and scared the heck out of me.

"Somebody is in my room," she yelled.

I got up and went to her room and found it empty. Our parents got up, and I went outside. The tree was the only thing near her window. We searched the house for intruders and again, came up empty. Our mother called the Pundit in India, who is considered a priest or a High holy man, He advised my parents to either cut down the tree or close my sister's bedroom window. My parents were not taking any chances, so they had the tree removed.

Even today, a guru, Vasant Vijay Maharaj, motivates me to learn more every day and understand spirituality through his teachings. Being a Maa ka Bhakt (devotee of goddess), he spent ten years without clothes in Himalayas meditating and worshipping the goddess and attaining nirvana. His teachings have made me even more blessed. I am very thankful to him even though I have never met him in person. His words are pure bliss in my life.

I say all of this to say, that sometimes life can throw challenges at you that seem to make no sense on the outside, but in reality, they have a profound impact on our lives. While our faith may be tested from time to time, we are never alone.

We cut the tree down to ensure my sister's spiritual safety. The Pundit knew, sitting far away in India, exactly what was happening to our family. We were under spiritual attack. He told us that certain souls go after young men and women. Sadly, one look at today's newspapers tells me that some of those same spirits take human form and stalk the streets in search of our youth to use and abuse them in such horrid ways.

My Grandmother and other elders in India are gone now, but they shared their sage advice with us on countless occasions. Not only to quiet our hunger for knowledge, but also to prepare us for the world at large. They loved us enough to pave the way, but also fill us with age-old knowledge that may seem foolish to some, but has saved my family time and time again.

One of the many bits of wisdom the elders gave us matched up with the wisdom of many cultures about the protection of the women. For instance, in my culture, it is important to never let a young girl go outside at night with loose hair or wearing a strong perfume. This is because it can attract a lot of energies and not all of them are kind.

Other warnings we grew up with included hair hygiene. When the hair is washed, it must be kept loose to dry. Negative energies are attracted to such hair to a greater extent. When such unfastened loose hair rubs against each other, due to friction, a flowing form of *Raja-Tama*, a predominant energy, is generated within the hair that can attract even more negative energy which can affect a person on so many levels.

The Older generation from India who has transcended has left behind so many things for us to understand and learn from them. Some may seem a bit antiquated or out of step with the times, but deep down those old-world values are the backbone of many cultures. The elders' wisdom matter even more so in this day and age where the hunger for knowledge and the wide consumption of inaccurate knowledge is harmful. When the world is filled with such darkness and the hunger for self-perseveration eclipses human compassion, human decency, I think of my grandmother and all those who have come before me. I am comforted by their wisdom and share it wherever I can. I'm smiling as I write this because eventually, I will take my place among the elders and share what I have learned. Perhaps, with this book, in my own small way, I am doing just that.

6

HUNGER ONLY FOR LOVE

I LOOK AT MY FEET
Walking the distance towards my love
Which is much more than I realize
Tranquilizing me with such pain
Hypnotizing me with evil ways

HUNGER ONLY FOR *love*

SIMPLE SWEET EYES *saying the words*
Flying high but below the reality
Those free birds
Two steps ahead
Yet still months and months away
Only one thing this heart needs to say
I miss you and

HUNGER ONLY FOR *love*

. . .

AHEAD IN TIME
Deepest oceans can be filled with my tears
Fiercest fire can be cooler than my desire
Inside, I'm invisible to the visible ones above
The creature lies inside
And it hungers only for love

POWERFUL MIND
Crazy coincidences
Insanity unexplained
Glorious eyes nowhere to be found

THEY ALL HUNGER *only for love*

7

LAY YOUR HANDS ON ME

MY GRANDFATHER IS MY GUARDIAN ANGEL. NOW I KNOW WHAT YOU'RE thinking. Earlier, you mentioned a *woman in white* and now you're saying your grandfather is one. Just how many do you have?

Well, believe it or not, I have a few and so do you. Sometimes we call them friends or soulmates. Other times they are strangers who offer a kind word or a listening ear just when you need it most. Each of us, alone, has a village of people ... of guardian angels looking out for us who care about our comings and goings.

My grandfather is one of those special people.

I never had a chance to meet him on this earthly realm, but I know that he's with me and like a true Dad, he's still looking out for his daughter, my Mom. She once told me something that has stuck with me. Her father had passed away a month before I was born. He wanted to be here to see me, but sadly, that was not part of his path. Needless to say, my mother was depressed because he was now with the angels, gone from this place. I was born January 24th mere weeks after his death in December.

She told me that while she was recovering in the hospital with me beside her, the mixture of joy and pain threatened to consume her. And at that moment, a gust of wind came, and she felt her father's hand across her forehead the way he had done so many times when he was alive. He whispered to her in Hindi, "I'm here. I'm always going to be around."

Mom still believes that her father came to bless the both of us. A Pundit told her, "Every single human being on this planet has guardian angels." No matter where you come from, everyone has them to guide and provide tender care when needed. She told me that my grandfather is *my* guardian angel. And I believe her. He protects me while I'm driving. He protects me while I'm out and about. I received clarity from this that if someone has passed beyond the veil and away from this earthly realm; just know that they're still around and in some ways, within you. They look on with pride when you achieve, and they hold you close when you grieve. In my heart and mind, my grandfather is one of my powerful guardian angels and someone that you love very much is your guardian angel, too.

So from that experience and others, I know about protection, and also embrace my earth angels.

Sometimes we're closer to our mothers than our fathers. Not to say that my father was distant or anything like that, but when I was growing up, especially during high school, he was always busy working, making a good life for us. Whatever I wanted whether it was a video camera, a bike, or anything like that, my father always managed to bring home for me and my sister. But he also gave us other things that were intangible and just as important. I carry them with me in every fiber of my being—like love and loyalty and an example of how a man should care for his family emotionally, physically, and spiritually.

My Mom was always home, making sure we had a solid presence, a wonderful atmosphere, and support. She worked too, but she always made time for us. I am proud to call myself a Mama's Boy. She was my first friend, my biggest fan, and my staunchest supporter. I would move Heaven and Earth to see her smile. I was, and still am, very close to my mom.

When I became a little bit older, I spent more time with my dad. My dad is a musician and singer and the main one who encouraged me to pursue a career in films and television. "You have to do this, my son. If it is your dream, then you must pursue it."

IT NEVER CEASES to fill me with a blushing pride when he shows me a small picture in the newspaper or a magazine and he boasts "Oh, my God, my son is in the newspaper."

I am a replica of him and any topic in a conversation that comes up, he always finds a way to steer the conversation to something about me. I am convinced that if there were buttons on his shirt they would pop off because his chest would swell with pride. Like my mother, my dad supports me, gently reminding me that I can achieve whatever I put my mind to. My mom does too, but my dad is more vocal proclaiming to the world: "He is my son, and he is capable of accomplishing more than even he realizes!"

When I travel to India, some family members and friends say that I look more like my mom, but when I see pictures of my dad, whose family is in Punjab, I favor them as well. Members of his family have aged, but they remember what he looked like in his youth. When I walk into their homes, they say, "Ah, Sudesh is here." Then they correct themselves and say, "No, this is his son." If another relative walks in and will say, "Oh, my God. It's like Sudesh has come. Same features, except a little bit of mustache."

Honestly, I'm like him in some ways, but in others, we differ. I am into fitness and became "buff", but that's mostly the only difference. It's funny how I meet those people in Punjab and they are so shocked, and it's a pleasant thing.

Having supportive parents and family can be a rarity for some. My advice in that situation is simple. Find your family. If they are not blood-related find others who are earthly connected to you. Cheer for them as much as they cheer for you. People are out there waiting to connect with you and support you. You deserve that. We all do. And it doesn't require fame or looks, or even money to find that connection. You are worthy, all on your own, of acceptance, support, and love. Love hard and fight even harder for each other and let the rest fall away.

8

THE QUENCH OF A THIRSTY HUMAN

DRAW YOUR ATTENTION TO MY LIPS
   See me licking them
   See them closed
   See them talking precious words that reveal too much
   The quench of a thirsty human

WHAT DO *you think it is she'll say?*
   It's not water, it's not the wind or fire
   So enlighten me with your vision
   As I search the night blindly

INTO THE BEAUTIFUL *gardens of eternity*
   Where the roses never die
   They reincarnate themselves
   Their fragrance is around me all the time

I LOOK *at love that has died many centuries ago*

Creeping shadows under my spell
But they don't listen to me

I CRY *like the way I haunt*
  I'm just a victim
  So understand I'm thirsty for your love
  And please don't taunt me
  You still don't know
  Because you aren't listening
  I'm thirsty for your love

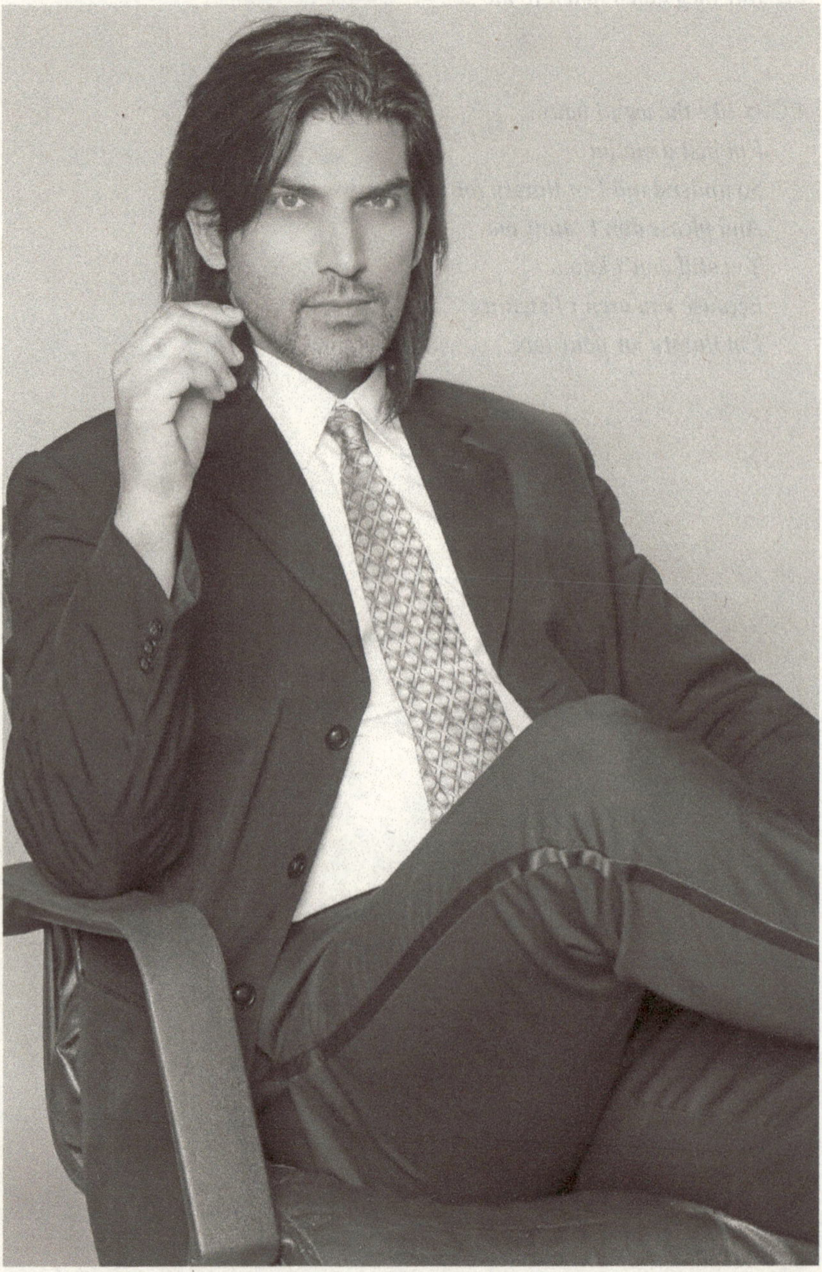

AIR (PAVAN)

1

THE BLESSING IS THE LESSON

GRIEF IS A FUNNY THING. FOR SOME, IT IS HEAVIER THAN LEAD WEIGHING down every part of the bereaved person's being. For others it is a feeling that's lighter than air and ebbs and flows like a gentle breeze. It may be destructive, wiping away normalcy and all a person ever knew on this side of the earthly realm. But we endure and move beyond it because in the end, grief is love turned inside out. Love that has no place to land.

My grandmother was another great love of my life, and for her, I was her life. My relationship with both of my grandmothers was very strong. I had an amazing connection with my maternal grandmother. But with my dad's mom, I was her entire world.

In an Indian family, for a grandmother, the grandson is very important. The son is important too, but they always say that if the father is a hundred dollars, the grandson is like a million. If my grandmother would turn on the television, she would only look for me. Any television advertisement came on, she would shush the others in the room because "her Vikkas would come on any second now". She passed about ten years ago or so. I remember very clearly the day my uncle called me when I was in Bombay and said, "Your grandma is not doing well. She's not going to make it. You must come as soon as possible."

I took the next flight to Delhi that very night. When I arrived, she was sleeping, but my uncle pulled me aside and informed me that she was not going to survive and that she had been suffering in those last days. Her breathing was shallow, and she constantly moved from left to right with pain. From the moment I entered the house, she settled down and slept through the night only because I believe, she was waiting for me. Around eight that morning, my uncle shook me by the arm and said, "Vikkas, you have to come down now." By the time I made it I made it downstairs, Gramma was tossing and turning in bed once more.

My aunt went to her and whispered, "Vikkas is here."

All of Gramma's labored breathing stopped. Her pain seemed to stop. She turned, opened one eye and reached out to me. I bent down, and she touched and blessed me. She gave me many blessings in the last few moments of her life, and I remember telling her how much I loved her. She gently massaged my head, brushing my hair through her hands as she said her goodbyes before the pain washed over her once more. I saw her take that last breath.

My world stopped, my heart broke, and I must confess something sacred. I asked God to give five to ten years of my life to my grandma so she could stay a little longer. As I write this, I think of an earlier passage I wrote about 'a world of goodbyes and a galaxy of hellos'.

Some goodbyes hurt worse than others.

And again, poetry became my saving grace where I wrote a couple of poems about death and life and other things. After my grandmother saw me, blessed me with that last breath which left her body, she was at peace. I have never seen anything like this or experienced this kind of pain before in my life.

Call it coincidence if you like, but I know that she waited for me. That should tell you the power of love. She was ready to go, long before I received that call from my uncle. My grandmother held on because she knew it was important for her to lay that final touch of her hand or her blessing on my head. She stayed long enough to remind me that she loved me for all the days to come when she wouldn't be able to say the words to me face to face.

That's how love works and how grief plays its very important role. Both remind us to treasure life and live in the moment. Selfies and photos are nice, but real, honest human connection overshadows technology any day of the week. Put down those cellphones and have the conversation. Experience a family tradition with your eyes instead of a camera lens. Life moments are fleeting. Enjoy it while it lasts, because it all ends sooner than any of us would like, and we can never go back. Love while you can. Live while you can. The present ... the greatest gift of your life is now. Right now.

With my grandmothers

My family knew my grandmother was dying. They knew her spirit was probably gone a day before, two days prior, waiting in limbo in two different dimensions. She was holding onto her breath. Like she had said, "I have to stay, because I have to see him."

Don't waste it dear friends. Tell people that you love them today. Give them their flowers literally and figuratively. Love them now because tomorrow is not promised.

If I had been here in America when she passed, there would have been so much regret and pain that I carried. The fact that I dropped everything to go, comforts me to this day. When my uncle and aunt called for me, I didn't say, "I'm too tired. I traveled all this way." I got up right then. And my aunt said the right words which brought on an amazing response. I could have just been in the room, but she said what was needed to bring my grandmother to where she wanted to be; to do what she had to do for me. I know now it's not about the people who leave, it's who they leave behind.

We grieve. We long for more time with the people who pass away, but know this, the pain changes. After a while it doesn't hurt to see the pictures or catch their scent in an article of clothing. The pain becomes nostalgia and the good memories return. Getting to that point hurts because life won't be the same. But it moves on. In time, so will you. And you won't forget them, and they don't forget you. You're just doing the one thing they loved most about you. In truth it is the best and only way to remember them.

You live.

My grandmother is not in pain anymore. She's not worried about anything. She's transitioned. She left me with her life and legacy. That was most important. When she reached out, and I looked at her and said, "I love you." She just blessed me all the way. This is how we all should go—loving and knowing that we are loved.

To my grandmother, it didn't matter that I was once that skinny little boy, the one who was bullied and mistreated, or the one that people outside of my family did not appreciate. She didn't know I would become the person I am today. She loved me even in my most vulnerable state; even with my insecurities and doubts. That's the thing that I will always carry with me, because that was extremely important for me to know.

Your frailties and insecurities do not define you. You are perfect just as you are, and the ones who truly love you revel in the joy of that fact. Nothing else is required. You are enough. You are enough simply because you are here. You are the answers to someone else's prayers simply because you draw breath.

To some, the passages between my poems may not make a lot of sense. Understand that I'm opening up with these points to tell my story through the written word. I'm reliving my pain and all this love through these poems, and I'm grateful to be sharing this with the world, and with you, most of all.

One of my biggest regrets is when my maternal grandmother passed away, I was not there. When we received the call, she was already on a ventilator. I have the video of my cousin telling my grandma, "Vikkas is watching", but she was already on that spiritual plane.

I didn't have that same connection with her that I had with my paternal grandmother. My love was obviously the same for both, but my mom's mom had a lot of other people she was worried about. She meant the world to me just the same. My *Biji*, (Paternal Grandma), Mataji (Maternal Grandma) both were such innocent, child-like, gentle souls and yet their deaths were an impactful tremor that radiated throughout our families.

I have seen elderly people suffer due to families withholding food and proper care because the focus is on money. That kind of greed is disgusting and shameful. I was hurt and used to cry hearing how mistreated some of the most vulnerable people in the world have endured. So many blessings are not bestowed upon the younger members of the family because our mothers, grandmothers, great grandmothers are subjected to people who no longer see them as valuable and precious.

There is a special place in hell for people like that. There is good karma and bad karma, all of it gets revisited to us in this life. Only foolish people fight, argue and destroy families because they are thinking only about money. None of our elders should be worried about their next meals. None of them deserve to be mistreated; especially when they have given so much to us already.

All of the women in my life are powerful. My sister, Megha, everyone in the world says that we look like twins. But my sister is my soulmate. People misunderstand when I say this because most believe that soulmates are only for romantic relationships. That is not the case.

Twin flames are thought to be one soul split into two bodies, soulmates are simply two separate souls that are linked spiritually. And believe it or not, people may have more than one soulmate in a lifetime. God is the perfect orchestrator. He gave me my beautiful parents, my loving mom and my loving dad and the miracle that is my compassionate sister. The way I express so many things, whether it's passion, compassion, caring, nurturing, that make me who I am, my sister is always part of it. She's always been here; even when I was in India struggling to make a career for myself on stage and in film. My sister took care of the house, she took care of my parents and became the protector of the house.

I always say, what a woman can do on this planet, a man could never think of. A man cannot surpass a woman's power and purpose. No freaking way. Not possible. A woman exists on a higher plane. A woman is always going to have that power. The Durga goddess that we worship, is a strong Deity. She lives in the women I'm surrounded by.

2

A GODDESS LIKE MOTHER

LOTUS PETALS ON HER DIVINE FEET
The whole universe conspires to meet HER
A rainbow like an umbilical cord
All my fears, my anxiety, my tears, my worries
In her heart she stored
It can only be my mother
Her sweet honest kind eyes and smile like no another
A Goddess like Mother
She put me in her arms when I was a baby
I held her hands as a toddler, then a teen
I walk with her as her eyes have become a little bit hazy
Her every breath is a blessing to me in my life
May God take away my years and give it to my mama
Divine paths where the peacock sings
Blessings to her as abundant as the joy she brings
My mother, the divine, sent in human form

3

LOVE LOST AND FOUND

T O SAY THAT A WOMAN IS THE EMBODIMENT OF A MIRACLE IS AN understatement. A woman has the power to give birth. Men play a pivotal role too, because he has that seed. I'm not discounting men's roles in the great scheme of things. Women actually carry, nurture, and form that life for those nine months as everything comes together— nervous system, organs, all of those things. Come on, be honest. If we had to depend on guys to carry a child, there would be no people on the planet, right? No people at all.

Women lay down their lives and some have lost their lives to bring that life on planet earth. And if I haven't said it before, then allow me to say it now very loud and very clear: You are goddesses. You are amazing. You are up there.

I remember the time my sister gave birth. Oh, my goodness gracious, the level of love and respect I have to give her for that act is beyond measure. They called us when she went into labor. We rushed to the hospital and waited outside until Krrish was finally here.

My parents held him first. When my turn came, I was very scared, really, because he was so tiny. I remember thinking, *How can he be a whole human being; it's such a tiny little thing?*

I LOOK AT HIM NOW, and I am so amazed. How time flies! One moment I was holding this warm precious bundle; then with what seems like the blink of an eye, he's freaking six years old and working on his black belt in karate. He prays to Lord Shiva, and Durga Maa faithfully. He chants his mantras before sleeping every night.

Krrish shares my love of Superman, but he also loves James Bond, Thor, Spider Man, and all the superheroes that one can imagine. In Bollywood, his favorite actor and the dance moves he copies, is no other than Salman Khan.

He is the only grandkid in our house, so he is a bit spoiled. In my mind, that just means that he is well loved. He still manages to be very respectful. He prays every night. He thanks God for giving him all the things he has in life-parents, etc. He is truly a one-of-a-kind kid. He willingly shares his toys. He's good at his studies and does martial arts. He's so soft-spoken and he's always, always 24/7, smiling. Krrish is a very old soul. We are all blessed to have such a good boy. He texts every day as I am his Mamu (Uncle). He sends photos of James Bond and Shiva and now he has started painting as well. He is six going on eighteen.

I guess you could say I am a proud uncle and a very grateful brother because my sister, my twin, my soulmate gave this incredible gift to our family in the form of my nephew. I live for the day that I would have the privilege of finding that special someone in my own life that I will share my heart and my seed with to create a family of my own.

My sister married the greatest guy, Sam, who was actually my best friend first. And like all brothers of younger sisters, I nearly pummeled him because I did not want him to be with my Megha. I was always overprotective and did not know or think that Sam's intentions towards my sister was to get married.

All in all, he proved himself to be a good and true friend and an even better brother-in-law, anyone could ever have. I see where my nephew gets many of his traits. Sam is a kind, gentle, soft-spoken soul. I wish I was as gentle as he is at times.

I think it's harder to find a soulmate than it is to find a twin flame. Twin flames are the way you learn your lessons. Most of my relationships were all just flames that burned me out. I've been through several encounters over the years, and it is only now that I can write about love with the halting respect that it deserves. I wrote about it as a boy as evidenced in some of the poems in this book. As a man, having experienced more of this life, I realize that for all the pain there was love. While it ended however it did, I wouldn't change a thing. I lived and loved some remarkable people. If life lasts, I will again.

Today, I am one of the top romance cover models, hopefully

inspiring passion in those who read the books, to believe in love as I do. Perhaps, by falling through the pages and living vicariously through the characters, they can escape, for a time, the challenges of life and get swept away in an adventure.

I have experienced love. I've had a few girlfriends and it was all about love, but not the deep kind. Sparks are lovely, but true love, that's a whole different thing. It's like an inferno that occurs between two people, and it consumes them body and soul. The same way a welder's torch takes two separate things and joins them together to make something new, something lasting. Something that is better than forever—like my nephew or your children and someday, yes, someday, even mine. Brahma The Creator smiles!

There was a girl that I was dating in India, she was pure love. It was all about love and care with her. I was already an affectionate person, and with her I became more so. Holding hands and talking about how I felt was as natural as breathing. I never cared or bothered about what the public would say because I truly loved her.

She showed me the wonders of Bombay and took care of me in the same loving and gentle manner, like a little baby gets taken care of by its sweet mother. We used to work out at the gym together and for a time, we were happy. She had the most wonderful parents who loved me, and mine loved her.

But as in books and life, sometimes things fall apart.

4

YOUR LOVE IS FADING AWAY

THEY THINK OF ME AS A PASSING WINE
>   Lots to taste but nothing to feel
>   Am I forgiven for such a crime I didn't commit?
>   Somewhere you'll see I was helpless to deal

YOUR LOVE WAS FADING AWAY
>   Will you tell me to stay?
>   Under your pillow you'll find my broken wings
>   Don't keep hope from the stars as thoughts become things

THE BEAUTY in holding my lover's hand
>   To caress my lover's each and every hair strand
>   Only if they could understand
>   They love I feel and the dreams I have planned

THE DAY that I have been waiting for a long time
>   When the minutes itself deceive as they pass by

I am sorry this is no fault of mine
And it all happens with no reason or rhyme

OPEN *your eyes and ears*
  Reach for me since I've been crying for years
  Life isn't fair, but it's one well lived
  Just when our love grew and I had more to give

LOVE HURTS SO *bad that my heart is bleeding*
  All the wonderful things from me that you're needing
  Don't be surprised to see me
  Be even more surprised if you don't
  Your love fading away

5

DREAMS HAVE A HEAVY PRICE TO PAY

WHEN YOU LEAVE YOUR HOME
> And you're all alone
> You travel to the other corner of the world
> The lights were on
> The camera was rolling
> And even the straightest hairs were all curled
> They all thought time was their father
> When mother nature-controlled dreams in their pockets
> They lied and wasted my time as if it was all in their dockets

DREAMS HAVE A VERY *heavy price to pay*
> *In exchange of dreams coming true they wanted your body and soul*
> *They could care less about the mind*
> *People who sold their soul became very big stars*
> *I kept mine and was left behind*
> *I picked up the shattered glass of my soul*
> *The water that was spilled*
> *And no cameras to roll*
> *Everyone spoke in a similar manner*

Just like we stand for the Star-Spangled Banner
Too many fireworks but not enough fire
Just like I left behind my last burning desire
The price was too heavy
And my soul is not for sale

6

WHERE DID OUR LOVE GO?

SHE'S MARRIED NOW, THE LOVE I SPOKE OF BEFORE. I ALWAYS THANK HER for my journey in India when I went in 2001. She helped me in ways I can't even explain. I am grateful for our time together. I am a better person for having known and loved her. Who knows? Perhaps in some small measure, she is better for having known and loved me. Isn't that what life is about? Learning from one another so that we become our better selves is love in its truest form.

During my time in India, I fed the poor and needy. I also became a supporter of the blind girl's orphanage there. I have always said *a poor person's mouth is God's pocket*. So, the more I help others, the more blessings I have. I can't see the Creator on this plane of existence, but I can serve Brahma by taking what I've been given and sharing them and the proceeds I gain from them with the world. What better way to share my love is there?

Brahma, The Creator smiles, indeed.

Romance covers using VikkasZone.com stock photos

(Photo taken with author Naleighna Kai at a romance book convention)

Strong colours and eclectic patte
for the man who likes to dare, v
sometimes just wants to let it a
hang out
Photographs by Harsh Man Ra

the bold
and the
beautiful

FEATURED IN MANY MAGAZINE

SKY / SPACE (AAKASH)

"Souls recognize each other by the way they feel, not by the way they look"—Dolores Cannon

ADS I SHOT FOR IN BOMBAY

1

THE DREAM REALIZED

WHEN I SIGNED A CONTRACT FOR MY FIRST FILM, IT WAS THE HAPPIEST DAY of my life. After shooting in Mauritius for a month, and then seeing myself for the first time as a lead actor on that big screen, my heart stopped.

films shot
in India

My parents were the happiest I had ever seen them. I can't describe the feeling. My hard work landed the part by meeting people, struggling, going on buses or rickshaws for auditions, and being hungry sometimes. The life of a starving artist. Now that's a whole different story.

It's strange how you can come so far and love so much and still find pockets of darkness within the world. In my travels to India and Africa, I always took time to feed the poor.

Where there is love, sadly there is also the opposite. I learned a lot about how people view those who are not like them. In India, as in other parts of the world, they judge others because they are overweight, too dark, too … something. As if a person's size or color is the entire content of their character. I don't give a damn about any of these things. We are all from the same source, like different rivers but leading to the main ocean.

2

MY FIRST FILM

SLEEPLESS AT NIGHTS ARE PART OF THE DESIGN
  Envisioning the day that I would be signed
  Like water flowing smoothly and rainbow-like streams
  The culmination of only one of my dreams

LIGHTS ACTION CAMERA, *he said*
  Straight to the cinema halls he led
  Larger than Life is what I saw
  Even though I was kind of raw

ALL MY FAMILY *rejoicing*
  Smiling and filled with such joy
  My first film

3

NEVER SHAME ANYONE

NINE MONTHS YOU'RE STUCK IN YOUR MOM'S WOMB
  After you come out, she gains a lot of weight
  Do you call her anything less than beautiful?
  People who shame others are soiled inside
  You must leave this sick mentality
  Never shame anyone
  Tomorrow, if your sister or aunt changes in physical form
  Will you love them any less?
  Don't try to race the dolphins just because you run on sand
  Your words are like fire and you will definitely burn your hands
  Only look down upon people if you're helping them up
  Your tragedy is your small mind
  Like a rat stuck on a running wheel
  You'd better heal
  So never shame anyone
  Respect all ethnicities
  Respect and love all women no matter their shape or size
  One day the sand might slip out beneath you
  And you will change your physical form
  Will you hope no one loves you any less?

4

ALL OF IT IS GOOD

IF YOU'RE KIND AND YOU'RE LOVING, THAT'S ALL THAT MATTERS. WHY should it be that if a person is Black, Brown or purple that you have to be cruel. We're all struggling to make it to the next moment, the next hour, and yes, in some cases the very next day. The journey is so much easier when we help each other along the way. We live in the most educated digital society of all time, and these outdated ideas have no place on the journey to spiritual wholeness or in our lives.

Sadly, for all the advances we make, some of the ugliest thoughts still prevail and twist the truth to suit its own twisted perception of what reality is. Media and society do not present women in the best light. Size zero women are no more beautiful than curvaceous women. Blonde is beautiful, but then again so is brunette and red-haired. The length or texture of a woman's tresses are like curtains. They do not add or detract from the beauty of the soul. And what if you are bald? Does that mean you have no value? Some believe that is true. I do not.

As I was growing up, I was always called skinny and ugly by other kids. For the young men out there, please know that the tiger inside you will awaken one day and you will go conquer the world. I used to watch bodybuilders in the gym, and then learned from the internet how to work out. I used to read a lot of magazines and books and learned how to transform myself into a dream body I always wanted. It took me couple of years, and then after I accomplished that goal, I started helping others.

WHEN I WAS EIGHTEEN, I wanted to expand my knowledge. I approached a bodybuilder who told me, "Why are you asking me? Go learn yourself". I walked away with a heavy heart because I wanted nothing more than to look bigger and fuller and knew that a little help from him would take me to the next level. Evidently, he must have realized the harshness of his words, because he came up to me, smiled and said, "okay, let's go. Let me teach you few things." I always want to help others achieve what they want in the gym since I learned this part of things the hard way.

I hold classes in the gym on how to eat right, how to bulk up, and how to get cut. Lot of these guys want fast results which I am against. If you want eighteen inch bulging biceps you must prepare accordingly. Of course diet plays a vital role. To this day, I am motivated so much more and when I see myself in the mirror. I'll say that I want more perfection and more agility. So I go right back in the gym and train hard each day, six days a week Not to mention I love playing racquetball four times a week. I have always said, "The gym is my girlfriend". That is because, it takes care of me mentally and physically.

"My Gym Is
My Girlfriend!"

Brahma created a world full of variety and all of it is good. Size matters in ice cream cones and cups of coffee. Not people. Beauty has little to do with the outside and everything to do with the inside. It breaks my heart that some women have to hide themselves because they don't look a certain way.

Plus size models are beautiful, and I've had the privilege of shooting with some of them for romance covers.

I UNDERSTAND LIVING A HEALTHY LIFESTYLE, but please don't tell teenagers that they have to be a certain way, or they won't be accepted. They have their entire lives ahead of them. So much of who they are, and will become, changes along the way. Teach them to accept who they are early on, then the world cannot make them feel less than who they are meant to be.

5

WASTING PRECIOUS TIME

WHEN THE SUN WAS OUT
> They said the moon is shining
> When the stars were shining
> They said good morning, stop whining
> Five plus five was never ten
> It was always eleven
> They wasted my precious time
> Months after months from midnight to seven
> They stole my jewelry and made me think I had lost
> Sleep with me to become famous
> That was cost
> Wasting precious time
> The Divine was always with me
> Devils disguised in human forms
> Angels were walking by my side
> I always heard the thunder
> I could always see the storms
> It was a battlefield just like the mahabharat (Epic Battle between good vs evil)
> And I was the one who won

understanding . . .

6

OUTWARD EXPRESSION OF LOVE

BEAUTY IS EVERYWHERE, AND WE SHOULD EMBRACE IT. IT'S NOT JUST ONE
particular color, ethnic group, size, status, or one particular way. This is
why I wanted to start shooting photographs with plus size models,
even when others said it was not something that would make me
successful.

I was shocked by some of the responses I received when arriving
on a set.

Some of them were genuinely shocked that I wanted to be
photographed with them. One model stepped back from me and asked
"You want to shoot with me? With the way I look at this size?" I
answered, "Yes, of course, I want to shoot with you. Heck, yes, I want
to shoot with you. You belong on the cover as much as I do."

The whole experience was a bit awkward at first, but in the end, we
captured the essence of love on film and I gained a new friend in the
industry. When I went to Atlanta, I shot with this beautiful woman
who did not understand the process and said, "I've never done this." I
replied, "It's the first time for me, too. It's perfectly fine."

I thought back to an earlier shoot and had to correct myself. It was
my second time, because the first one, I shot with a Filipino girl who
was really—oh, gosh, she was so absolutely gorgeous. Beautiful. I told

her, "You are a stunning woman." She was like, "Really? Thanks, Vikkas."

Things became a little bit awkward there, too.

In photoshoots, we must create these romantic scenes. In many ways, it is like an actor preparing to be on screen. You establish a rapport with the person you are working with. You build a level of trust that, if done correctly, will be perfectly captured on film. When it's done right, no words are needed. It's just two people representing characters in a book who love each other and let the rest fall away.

Unfortunately, some of the models would look everywhere except at me. They could not look me directly in the eyes and part of me understood why. The eyes are truly the windows to the soul. Love comes in that way. We risk vulnerability and all that we are, all that we fear, and the fathoms of pain that well beneath. To risk that with someone we love is hard enough but to risk it with someone new is even more dangerous.

Finally, I had to say, "Tell you what, I won't look at your eyes. I will look in between your eyes. The trick is to look in the middle of the eyes. Don't look *at* my eyes. Look directly at the middle of the eyes. Can we do that?"

They said, "Yes." Things were much better, and those photos are some of the most amazing ones I have ever done.

It doesn't matter that one person is from one way of life and the other is from another way of life. All that matters is love. It's what artists try to capture in oils and singers with a lyric or their voice. Poets and writers spend lifetimes trying to capture it on the page and maybe pocket a little of it for home.

That is what this book is about. The expression of love and all of the different emotions that I've been through in order for others to understand who I am, and how this has helped me to grow. That's why this book couldn't just be poems. I had to share my experiences as well. How does one accurately see the measure of a poem without understanding—in some way—the poet that put pen to page?

7

REMEMBER US

ONCE UPON A TIME
Remember us
Growing up in the mists of childhood
Playing in the shadows of the rain
Going through the anguish and pain
We gained sweet friendship
The little crushes
In our big hearts
One day
We had to be apart
Loneliness is never forgotten
Even if we are seven oceans apart

8

LOST DREAMS

You are so far
  It's the truth

YOU ARE *an illusion*
  A most unwelcome intrusion

MY EYES WANT *to see you*
  It's a request

I WANT *to say I love you*
  It's my love

I TOTALLY MISS *you*
  It's my heart

. . .

VIKKAS BHARDWAJ

LOST *in your love right now*
    It's denying us being together

I'S *a photograph*
    Golden moments forever

IT'S *my memory*
    Other girls want to create love

HOLDING *you tight*
    Coming back with all my might

IT'S MORE *than fantasy*
    Kissing you passionately

IT'S *my desire*
    I feel your love

IT'S *my feelings*
    I love you

IT'S JUST *me*
    Your lover
    Lost in this dream

HOPING *everything I envision*
    Is more than what it seems

9

HEART: MY FIRST KISS

HEART: MY FIRST KISS

THE FIRST TOUCH *of your hands*
  Like walking in time of the sands

AMUSE *me with your smile*
  Enlighten me with your eyes

DON'T DROP *those tears*
  The past of the future is to fear

IN THIS DRAMA *of the world*
  Love is much like a hidden pearl

DECEIVING *hearts burn in the light of the sun*

VIKKAS BHARDWAJ

A fairy tale to the conclusion

DREAMS *to start the story*
   Broken angels have a lot to worry

CUPID SHOOTS *the arrow*
   This time it goes straight and narrow

IT GIVES *you the light*
   Like a bullet fired and takes your love out of sight

MY HEART IS STOLEN
   Locked in the prison of eternity
   My deepest feelings shattered for all to see

REMEMBER IF YOU LOVE, *then carry your tears*
   Like a wallet in your pocket lost for too many years

KEEP IT ALL IN, *but don't lose your heart*
   That first kiss can tear you apart

10

DETOURS IN THE LIVES OF KNIGHTS AND YOUNG MEN

As I sit to pen these pages, I realize that my memoir, my book of poetry has come full circle. In the beginning of musings for this book, I spoke of my first actual girlfriend when I was seventeen years old, turning eighteen, living in California. I was seeing her for a couple of months and used to take the bus where she lived. I likened myself to a knight traveling a great distance to see his lady fair. The only difference was that I was on a bus traveling to where she lived.

During that time, my family and I had to take a trip to India, for what was only supposed to be a two weeks trip to get our passports done. The U.S. Embassy had called us to our place of birth for necessary documents. So, my family had to make the trek to India. We were supposed to go, get our paperwork completed, passport done and come back within two to three weeks max. We didn't know that we were going to be stuck there for a whole nine months.

Life does have a way of making detours in the lives of knights and young men.

11

LIGHTS OUT

A FRIEND OF MINE CALLED ME WHILE I WAS IN INDIA AND SAID, "THE GIRL you were seeing, she's seeing somebody else already."

And with the words, it was like my whole world came crashing down. I wrote poems and wept bitterly over the love lost, and the life I dreamed that we would have together. Weeks became months and her question, "Are you coming home?" was like a knife in my skin. I was oceans away, but it felt so much further to me back then.

I wrote the poem *It's Time to Cry* because she left me without even telling me. I had to find out through someone else. Like, that's just cold, the kind of heartbreak no young guys ever want. I couldn't take it. That was the first experience I had drinking alcohol, as well. My uncle, Anil chacha, said, "You're sad," and got me some beer for the first time.

I turned eighteen, was stuck in Delhi, drinking beer, feeling sad, and writing poems. My favorite poets alive or dead were raising a glass with me in sympathy—at least in my imagination.

One bottle of beer was all it took for me to sleep the entire next day away. That was some strong ass Indian beer! I wasn't thinking about sadness or pain. It was lights out.

When I woke up, more poems came.

12

EVERY SILENCE IS A SCREAM

HOPE EARTH EXPLODES
Yet leaves me behind to create
There's more to life than living to write
So what if God is in a box
So what if the angels are drunk
So what if the fairies are selling dreams
I am the buyer
I am the one
Now they're paying for their consequences
No one is the healer
No one is a deceiver
I sentence her to a place of never-ending return
Even hell is a place to burn
Read me like a book
Beg me forever
Every silence is a scream
Now don't shed tears of rain
You needed my love, but gave all of this pain
You made me love and now we both suffer
You stone-face coward

Humans only vision of you
Daydreams of you
Now I'm giving you a dose of your own nightmares
I'm destroying you through your memories
And through this treacherous mind of mine
Don't look into my eyes you'll see your fate
You should have been mine
But I didn't accept your lies
It hurt me then
But now I only hear your cries

13

SETBACKS AND HEARTBREAKS

WHEN I FINALLY RETURNED TO THE STATES, I HAD A CHANCE TO CONFRONT her. Even then the way I dreamt of our reunion was nothing like the love stories I read or imagined. Even after I explained to her that I planned to come back, but ended up stuck in India for a while, her mind was made up, and she had moved on. The place I held in her life now belonged to someone else.

That world of goodbyes and my galaxy of hellos was upon me. Throw in a few more setbacks and heartbreaks, and my journal and I became close friends. The love of my young life was gone, but I continued to write more poems and seek more spirituality as they came and comforted me.

After a year passed, my 'galaxy of hellos' stretched out before me in the form of new friends and a new girlfriend.

14

WHAT'S IN THE CARDS

I WAS STILL A LITTLE GUN SHY AFTER MY FIRST HEARTBREAK AND NOT really looking for something more but she, this new girl, came into my life at a time when I thought love just wasn't in the cards for me. She proved me wrong. I could wax on about new love and the flames of passion that ignited the world around us, but I think you already know a lot of amazing things happened as did other experiences that would shape my life.

15

SWEET PEACOCK'S EYES

THOUGHT I HEARD YOU CRYING
  Thought I dreamt you were trying
  To reach your destination
  Dying love yet infinity lovers
  Tears like ink on a paper
  Hope it covers writing words in a deceiving manner
  fantasy thinking, unreal minds
  But somethings real
  That's chosen
  Sweet peacock's eyes
  Redness below them
  Put the fear aside you only dance when the rain pours
  I only cry when there's paper to write
  Wish I had many more doors
  To open
  To set me free

16

TAKE MY LOVE AND RUN

AFTER A YEAR AND A HALF OF BEING WITH HER, SHE SUDDENLY DECIDED that she wanted to move on and have different friends—boyfriends. Because she was young, right? Sometimes as much as being in love can be wonderful, heartbreak is waiting around the corner with a one-two punch that puts you flat on your back. You already know the sadness came in like waves crashing into the shore. And my thoughts started racing once more.

Wow, will this part of life ever end? Because here was the second most important girl in my life, and she essentially left me too. *What was it about me that they felt they could take my love, then run?*

17

___

SUN SHINES ON ME

DID YOU EVER WAKE UP IN THE MORNING
    And thank the sun for shining down on you and me

US LITTLE PEOPLE *waiting on the ground*
    Embracing the light and the sun's sound

SUN GOD DOESN'T CARE
    What you wear
    What you look like
    What color you are
    What nationality you are

RAYS *of light heals you within*
    Fold your hands
    And he blesses you to win

. . .

VIKKAS BHARDWAJ

LIFE ON EARTH
You feel cold or feel the heat.
From the solid ground beneath your feet

BE *thankful to the sun*
   Wake up early before he comes out
   Sun blesses you abundantly
   Without a doubt

SURYA MAHARAJA IS *the king (Surya Maharaja = Sun God)*

18

SNATCHERS OF YOUR INNOCENCE

LOVERS OF MY HEART
  I'm hiding in the wrinkles of your face
  Hidden Priceless jewels
  No other place
  When you are crying
  I hold on to your every tear
  Not to waste
  To keep, hold, and save
  Her precious sorrows,
    Nothing too grave
  I'm waiting for another storm
  I'll stop yours
  Who will stop mine?
  Lovers of my heart
  They are snatchers of your innocence

19

PLACING A BET ON LOVE

At this time in my life, I was really in a dark place. I was questioning everything about myself. If I were a sportsman, my batting average was at an all-time low. To recap, I was just over an experience, the first girl in high school who I was infatuated with who didn't care two cents about me. According to her, I was an ugly duckling. Then I met my first girlfriend, and she stomped on my heart because she refused to wait for me. Then my next moved on to greener pastures. One would think that if love were a person all on its own that I had offended them. Luckily for all of us, that isn't true or who would even attempt those fiery feelings of love at the risk of rejection again.

But life … actually, love has a way. It always has a way.

I experienced so many wonderful different things with her. Then one fine day she called me at work and said, "Vikkas, I need space." And I didn't see it then, but now as I am writing this book, I realize there was a gift in her goodbye. I put my energy into improving myself. Then after five or six years, I left for Bombay to pursue my dreams.

These poems are written pretty much at a young age, experiencing first love and the pain that comes when it ends. I do remember the good times, but sometimes they are overshadowed by that painful thrust at the end. I never expected my first love to break my heart the way she did. And then the next girl with whom I experienced all these amazing things, she also leaves. So to me, it felt like one painful loss after another.

20

WHEN I'M GONE

What will you do when I'm gone?
    Hope there is everlasting dawn

WHEN I WAKE *up in the morning*
    It was your smile I wanted to see
    But in this moment, you're not there
    When I long to show you how much I care

WHO WILL YOU HOLD?
    Who will caress you in their arms?
    Giving you the love that I once gave

ALL THE LOVE *I've given you causing so much pain*
    What will you do when I'm gone

I SAW *unborn children in your eyes*

Wanted to give you the moon, the world and the skies
I feel as if I am the Ghost of your city
My life torn
What will you do
When I am gone

Waiting to see you fix doors, fix roofs and fix sky
Finding if I am the smasher, smashing?
As if in a
What and what do
What I can give

21
_____

ANNIVERSARY

TODAY IS AN UNIMAGINED DAY
  Wanting to do all the things that make you stay
  Things are crystal clear no more
  Feelings in my heart open like a door

I WANT *to be back into your arms*
  Spellbound by your touch and charm
  Remembering when my heart touched the sky
  I couldn't imagine if you cried

COUNTING *tears for every day*
  When every emotion is like centuries away
  Hold me close and share my lonely heart
  Our worlds so close but yet so far apart

TODAY IS THAT SPECIAL DAY, *and I must express*
  Giving that love with no regrets

Like a little boy crying in his cradle
Being without you can be considered fatal

LIKE A SOLDIER LIVING *with a bullet inside*
These are the things that I try not to hide
I can feel the rain touching your skin
That matches the beauty you have within

THE ESSENCE *of you has so much love to give*
I can see the promise of the way we should live
I will never quench my desires somewhere else
My lover's lips on mine is always heartfelt

THE MEMORIES *of your hands on my chest*
Telling me the things you love best
Another year, another time and it all comes to this
Happy Anniversary and more years of bliss

22

CLOSURE

THE ANNIVERSARY POEM COMES FROM MY EXPERIENCE AND HOW IN ONE OF my relationships we always celebrated our anniversary. One month passed by. One-month anniversary. Then, two-month anniversary, six-month anniversary, seven-month anniversary. I used to give her chocolates and roses all the time because every day was a special occasion for us.

The money to buy gifts wasn't so much of a thing since I started working at one of my first jobs at a shoe store. I had also saved any money my parents gave me and rarely spent it on myself. My sister or mom would always get me what I needed. These wonderful loving women in my life made sure I had new shoes, clothes, cologne, and so many other things.

My family is so close that we always anticipate each other's needs. Everything we own we share with one another from cars to our home or whatever the other family member may need. I have received plenty of strange looks when I mention this in conversation. For all of the riches in the world, what do we really have if we can't share it with family or the ones we love?

I remember when I went on dates, I liked to make the girls smile, make them as happy as they made me. But for me a date is just getting to know someone. Only time spent in deep conversation yields the true value in any relationship.

Once, when a girl I was dating asked to split the expense for lunch. I laughed at the prospect. In my mind, it seemed like such a business transaction. Instead of two people enjoying time together, we would decide who would pay for the salad or the sandwich. I had to ask, do you mean, I will pay for my sandwich? And you will pay for your Coke and so forth?

I was appalled. Call me old-fashioned, but I do my best to take care of the women in my life. That includes paying for an entire meal or experience while we are out together. They deserve it for all the joy they bring to this world. If I can't spend money on the woman I take out, I should not be out with her in the first place.

When we all leave this planet, what are we taking with us? Property and money can be squirreled away in a casket but who does it benefit? Only your karma and deeds you do while here on this planet matter. It grieves me to see people fighting over material things when true family connection matters so much more.

Even with everything we put into the relationship, my last girlfriend left me a few years ago because she "Wanted to be alone".

And once again, I started wondering if maybe the planets, the stars, or the universe were conspiring to keep me away from that type of love that's written between the pages of the best romance novels. The kind of love that is legendary. We gave each other spiritual support, mental support, and she kept me happy all the time as she is a kind and a very giving soul herself. But a future together just wasn't in the cards.

Even though I was alone on my birthday, I came to the certain realization that no matter how much you love or do for anyone on this planet, at the end of it, the family that you are born into or the one you make here on earth is all that matters. They are the ones that will stand by you unconditionally.

Mostly everyone thought that I would get married to her, she was very kind and loving. She was a beautiful girl inside and out. I had asked her to marry me, but it was in a humorous way. My family loved her, but sometimes love isn't enough, and we have to move on.

It took me a while to understand, but now I know deep down that some people are only in your life for a short while. People have come into my life and conveniently walked out of it. Yet, I thought I remained the same. But upon reflection, they take a part of me with them, and I do the same, making us both change in some small way.

Whenever I look around at my family while we enjoy a meal, I am humbled and so honored to have them in my life. True family—birth or earth made—won't bullshit you. They won't take you for a ride. They won't waste your time. Family makes you realize that some people are gifted at giving lip service and no action. Family shows you, day in and day out, what love is supposed to be. They try their best to warn you of what love is not. And if ever I forgot those valuable lessons my family taught me, I had the displeasure of meeting a lot people on my journey from India to America to remind me.

My last relationship ended because she wanted to be free, but upon further thought, her departure from my life freed me. I took a spiritual journey to India. I didn't have to call in and check in on a girlfriend or have her check my every move. To coin an old advertising phrase from Southwest airlines, I was now free to move about the cabin.

I became free mentally, emotionally, and physically, to travel for a spiritual purpose. But I would not have been as comfortable making that journey if I was tied in an intimate relationship. That spiritual journey was extremely important.

Deep down, perhaps I knew she was not "the one". We became friends. We have done a lot of romance covers together and worked well together. She has amazing expressions and brings out the best in me in photo shoots. But her wanting to be free set me free.

The call I made to her before I left for India, that was closure. I had nothing, no more soul ties in that sense, which gave me the ability to concentrate on the lessons to be learned in the next part of my journey.

23

SPIRITUAL SCENT OF MY BODY

FROM CENTURIES AND CENTURIES, THE SOUL REMAINS THE SAME
    But the physical body keeps changing
    We embrace a spiritual scent that identifies us

OUR ANGELIC DUST *keeps enhancing with space and time*
    Like our words keep reincarnating with every rhyme
    I see you God
    Blessing me with spiritual scent that defines me

YOU COME *in my dreams you show me miracles*
    I can't understand one percent of it
    But I know you watch over me and my family
    Crafted by the spiritual scent of my body

WITH FOLDED *hands I pray*
    Always feed the poor the hungry and never go astray
    I've been searching for you, God, all my life

I love you Shiva with your beautiful Goddess wife
And the spiritual scent you leave in your wake

NINE PLANETS
> *Nine goddesses*
> *Nine months for baby to be born*

I ALWAYS SEEK *you in my third eye*
> *Like clothes to be worn*
> *I see you God with invisible eyes*

ALL THE LIGHT *I seek*
> *Keep me close to you as infinity flies*
> *I want the same parents*
> *Same sister in my next life*
> *I hope they can recognize me*
> *By the spiritual scent of my body*

24

THE NEW JOURNEY BEGINS

YOU HAVE TO UNDERSTAND THAT THAT JOURNEY AND THAT PATH I WAS ON with her, needed to end there. At the heart of things, I always ascribe and aspire to be higher on a spiritual plane. Our time together was over and there were no hard feelings. Like every season, they end at some point, in order to make room for something new.

After my Spiritual journey to Amarnath yatra in the city of Jammu and Kashmir, it didn't stop there. I went to Bombay to meet my dear friend Anjana who is yet another beautiful spiritual soul. When she visited us in California, we had the most amazing happiest times going to Hollywood and Laguna beach. She made me forget all my worries, honestly. She's the one I also experienced travelling to most of the holy temples of India. We went to Kolkata, South India, Delhi and Assam. Most wonderful experiences I have ever shared with anyone is with her. I am always grateful she took time out to make sure I visited all the places I wanted.

I used to always think that when a girl or woman left, I was dead inside. I always felt like the emotions were gone completely. Now I realize that they simply transformed. As we all do if we plan to successfully make our way through this life.

My reflections and experiences are on threads in the tapestry that is my life. They are selected highlights in poetry of the my growing up in New York, Los Angeles, and journeys to India. They are but small snippets of time on a continuing course that waxes and wanes like a river.

Some of this understanding is as old as Father Time and Mother

Nature. Mine is deeply rooted in a way of life that is peaceful and embraces many. When people say Hindu mythology in relation to the gods and goddesses I mentioned earlier in the book, please understand that it's an English word that was coined when India was under attack. It's never, ever mythology. It's always under Hinduism which some consider the oldest religion. But I would like to clarify, Hinduism is not a religion, it's a way of life. It's deep subject which I cannot explain in much detail here. No one taught me. Gods just come to you and while watching praying, either you connect with them or they connect to you. There are scriptures written and said that date back more than 10,000 years back. It's mind-blowing and fascinating and cannot be explained in a paragraph.

motivate and inspire you dear reader, to live. To love. To be unapologetically you.

And that is what I want for you. With my regard and sometimes

LORD SHIVA TEMPLE OF TRAYAMBAKESHWAR

Between these pages are the dreams, the desires, the motivation, the passion for life that carried me from childhood to this day. With these pages and the poetry that flowed from my pen, I hope to motivate and inspire you dear reader. To live. To Love. To be unapologetically you.

And that is what I want for you. With my rugged and sometimes abstract poetry, I hope you can find a sliver of yourself in the words and take comfort in them as I have.

Give yourself the permission to be free to find the thing that makes you happy whether it involves embarking on a spiritual journey or embracing a new hobby. The greatest adventure, the most important one you will ever go on is your journey into self. Mine those dark places in your soul. Get rid of old baggage and old ways of thinking. Cry those tears and laugh until your stomach hurts, but live until it's time to return to the infinite.

You are free.

TILL WE MEET AGAIN MAA

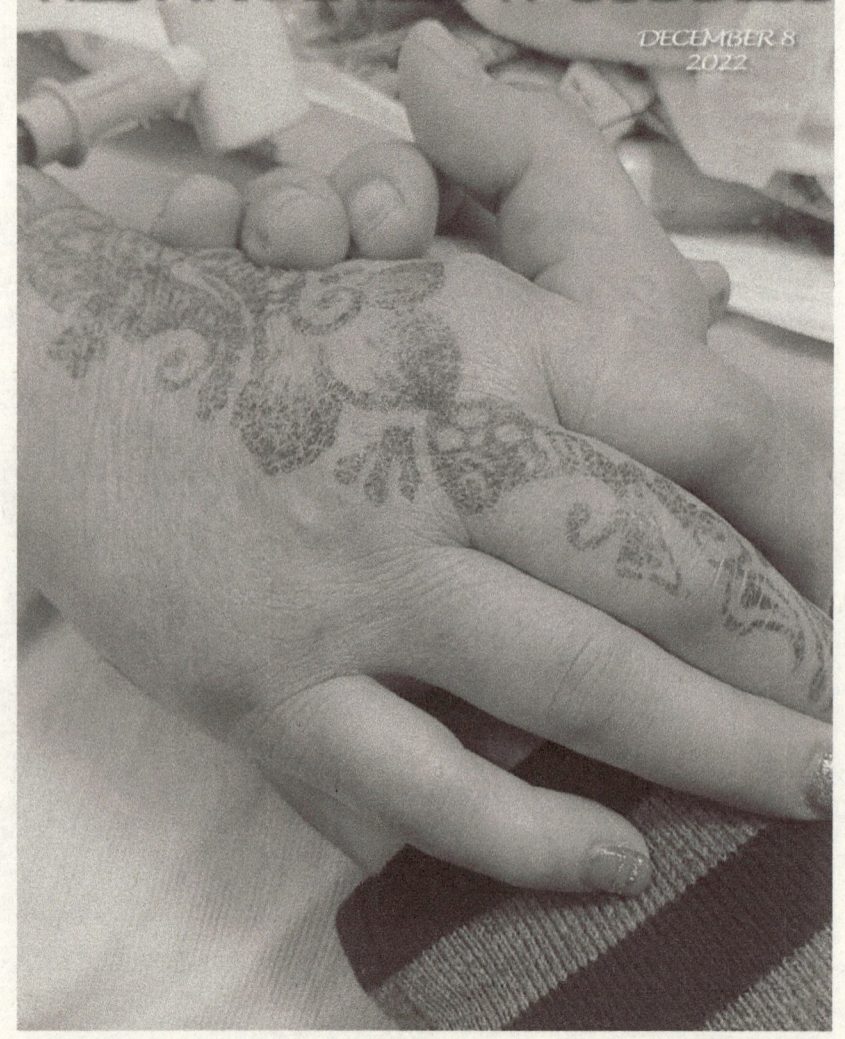

MY GRANDPARENTS FROM MY FATHER'S SIDE

ABOUT THE AUTHOR

Vikkas Bhardwaj is a Bollywood actor and international model who been in demand from the top fashion industry companies as far as Sri Lanka, Africa, India and the United States. His face has been a prominent fixture on the covers of magazines such as *GQ Asia*, and promotional advertisements for Ray Ban, Men's Health, Bazaar, and Health Mag. Though Vikkas had been a runway model for nearly a decade, and appeared in several soap operas and Bollywood films, including Classic Dance of Love, he switched gears and took the romance novel industry by storm a few years ago.

Since that time, he has graced the covers of more than five hundred novels at the request of *New York Times* and *USA Today* bestselling authors alike. Vikkas, who was born in New Delhi and raised in New York, now resides in Los Angeles where he is currently working on a novel that will motivate and inspire others to fulfill their dreams and desires and reach a level of success they never thought possible.

He credits his family with playing a major part in providing the foundation and backbone that allowed him to focus on reaching his level best. When he isn't in front of the camera, Vikkas
is raising funds for local and international charities that focus on helping children in need.
https://mrstaroftheworld.wixsite.com/vikkas
www.vikkaszone.com

CPSIA information can be obtained
at www.ICGtesting.com
Printed in the USA
BVHW071425260123
657206BV00018B/1078